Upshur Press
Fairfield, Iowa 52556

www.upshurpress.com

First printing (USA): November 1991
Second printing (USA): January 1992
Third Printing (Thailand): January 2006
E-Book (USA): March 2016
Fourth Printing (USA): January 2019

Design for third printing by Anthony and Meike

Library of Congress Cataloging-in-Publication Data
Stallone, Linda, 1947 –
The flood that came to grandma's house / written by Linda Stallone;
illustrated by Joan Schooley
p. cm.
Summary: When heavy rainfall from Hurricane Agnes causes
the Susquehanna River to flood, Grandma and Grandpa
abandon their home and flee to higher ground.
ISBN 0-912975-02-4: $14.95
1. Floods --Susquehanna River Valley -- Juvenile literature
2. Hurricanes -- Susquehanna River Valley -- Juvenile literature
3. Hurricane Agnes. 1972 -- Juvenile literature. [1. Floods.
2. Hurricane Agnes. 3. Hurricanes.] I.Schooley, Joan, ill.
II. Title
GB1399.4.S9S76 1991
363.3'493--dc20          91-33955
                 CIP
                 AC

# THE FLOOD THAT CAME TO GRANDMA'S HOUSE

Written by Linda Stallone
Illustrated by Joan Schooley

Dedicated to
Sally and Tony Stallone, the real Grandma and Grandpa of the story,
and to their grandchildren, Anthony, Maria, and Kiran, who needed to understand
what had happend to their Grandparent's home after it was flooded.

This printing is dedicated to the memory of Anthony, who skillfully redesigned this real life story
for yet another generation of children. Anthony's meticulous attention to detail brings out the humor of
Joan Schooley's brilliant illustrations and the perfect simplicity and truth of the story.

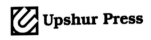 Upshur Press

This is Grandma and Grandpa's house.
They are sitting on their front porch
watching the rain come down.

The rain came one day…                    then two…

three days…                    then four.

It rained longer and harder than it ever did before.
The puddles got bigger.
The streams ran faster.
And the river rose… higher and higher.
Grandpa walked down to the river bank
to see how high the water was rising.
He saw the water coming up the bank and said,

*"If it doesn't stop raining,*
*the water will fill the river up so much*
*that it will spill over the ground*
*and flood the land on both sides of the river."*

Grandpa helped lots of people fill up bags of sand.
They stacked the sandbags on top of each other
all along the river bank.
They hoped the sandbag wall would hold the river back
where it was supposed to flow.

But the rain kept coming and the river kept rising higher.
The river got so strong and full of water that it was going
to push through the sandbag wall. Everyone left
the river bank to find safe places far, far from the water.

Since Grandma and Grandpa live close to the river,
they jumped into their car to drive far, far away.
But Grandma said, *"Stop! Stop! I forgot something."*
What do you think was so important?
Grandma's clothes? her jewelry? her photo album?

# Nope!

Grandma ran back for Vanilla,
the biggest, furriest, whitest cat
in the whole wide world.

So off they drove to a friend's house – too far away for the river to reach them.

Meanwhile…

the river broke through the sandbag wall.
Water flooded the streets.
Water started filling up the houses.

First the water filled Grandma's basement.
Then the water went up the basement steps and filled
the kitchen and the living room, getting higher and
higher, going up the stairs to the bedrooms.

Before long, the water went so high, all you could see
was the roof of Grandma's house.

But everyone was safe, far from their houses,
far from the flood, too far to get hurt by the water.

Soon the rain stopped,
and the river water went down down down
until water no longer spilled all over the ground.

The water was back in the river where it belonged.

Grandma and Grandpa went back to see their house.
What a yukky, muddy mess.
As the water went up and then the water went down,
everything in the house floated around.
Everything got all mixed up and broken.

The dirty river water left a thick layer of mud
all over everything the water touched.

… and the water touched everything in the house!

Grandma and Grandpa sure had lots of work
to clean up the mess. But many people came to help.
First, they threw everything that was in the house
out onto the street.

Bulldozers went up and down the streets, pushed all the piles
of muck onto a great big truck and took it all away.

Grandma's house was empty.
It took a long, long time to dry out.
It took a long, long, longer time to make it nice and clean again.
But everybody worked very hard.
The day finally came when Grandma and Grandpa
could live in their house again.

There they are now, sitting on the porch. The house is clean and they are glad to be back. This time I'll bet you can guess what they are talking about. Right! The Flood that came to Grandma's house. And they sure hope another flood never, never comes again!

• • •

Do you know anyone or anyplace that has been affected by a flood?
You can write about it here. Be sure to write your name and today's date.